Leprechauns
Never Lie

Written and illustrated by Lorna Balian

Humbug Books   Watertown, Wisconsin

Leprechauns Never Lie

First Copyright ©1980 - Abingdon Press

Copyright © 1994 Lorna Balian and Humbug Books

Fifth Printing 1994

This book is printed on acid-free paper in the United States of America

Library of Congress Cataloging in Publication Data
BALIAN, LORNA
 Leprechauns Never Lie.
 SUMMARY. Gram is ailing and Ninny Nanny, too lazy to care for their simple
 needs, says she'll catch a leprechaun to discover his hidden gold. Gram thinks
 it won't work – but does it?
 (1. Leprechauns–Fiction)   1. Title
          PZ7.B1978Le   (E)   79-25950

ISBN 1-881772-07-1
(Formerly ISBN 0-687-37110-4 and 0-687-21371-1)

MANUFACTURED BY INLAND PRESS
MENOMONEE FALLS, WISCONSIN, U.S.A.

For my grandson, Piep, with love

There was this old thatched hut nestled in a glen near the river.

Ninny Nanny and Gram lived there together.
Each had only the other and no more.
They lived simply on potato soup,
and their needs were few.

The thatch needed patching,
The potatoes needed digging.
The firewood needed gathering,
and the water barrel needed filling.

But Ninny Nanny was lazy, and Gram was ailing—
and there was naught but blathering between them.

Gram nagged, Ninny Nanny dawdled, and that was that.

The rain came drip-drop through the thatch.
The potato sack emptied.
The chimney pot grew cold,
and there was but a bit of rainwater in the barrel.

It came to be there was little to eat.
Just cold rainwater soup—pure and simple.

"Oh, woe is me! 'Tis starving we are," moaned Gram.
"What am I to do with such a lazy child?"

"Agh, Gram, hush your nagging!
I've been thinking to catch a leprechaun.
He's bound to tell where he's hidden his gold,
and 'tis rich for life we'll be," boasted Ninny Nanny.

"Is it raving you are, girl?
To capture a leprechaun is no easy thing!" said Gram.

"Aye, so I've heard tell," agreed Ninny Nanny,
"but we could make right use of a treasure, so I'll give it a try."

Well, it was as easy as tripping over a log, which is what happened.
Ninny Nanny was tramping about, looking every which where for a leprechaun,
when she tumbled head over petticoat and fell—plunk—
right on top of one of the wee fairy men.

He howled like a banshee and wiggled and waggled,
but Ninny Nanny had him firmly by the seat of his britches.
And that was that.

"Let me go!" shrieked the angry leprechaun.

"Sure, and gladly I'll let you loose, but I'll know first
where your treasure is hidden," said Ninny Nanny.

"Agh! 'Tis under the straw pile, but you've not the wit
to find it," grumbled the wee man.

"We'll see about that!" said Ninny Nanny as she carried him,
squirming and kicking, to show Gram her prize.
And wasn't she pleased.
They tied him firmly into a potato sack,
and Gram watched that he didn't waggle away—

while Ninny Nanny started pitching straw—this way and that.

"Sure, and 'tis witless and lazy she is,"
hissed the leprechaun to Gram.
"She'll find no treasure in the mess she's making!"

"I heard that, and you'll not fool me, Leprechaun!"
said Ninny Nanny, and she lifted the straw gently,
searched through it bit by bit,
and carried it up to the roof—out of the way.

Sure, and the whole of the straw pile was upon the roof,
and not a mite of gold to be found. And that was that.

"'Tis a liar you are, Leprechaun!" bawled Ninny Nanny.

"Agh! A liar I'm not! Hidden under the straw it was,
but I just now recall that the mice were nosing about,
so I moved it under the big oak tree
and covered it with branches," said the leprechaun.

"Stack the branches here by the door, Ninny Nanny,"
said Gram. "I'll sort through them for any stray coins."

Ninny Nanny carried and stacked the branches.
Gram examined every stick. The leprechaun scowled.

Ninny Nanny raked up the last few twigs
and found no speck of treasure under the tree.
And that was that.

"He's lying again, Gram!" howled Ninny Nanny.

"Agh! A liar I'm not! Hidden under the tree it was,
but I remember now that I moved it to a safer place,"
mumbled the leprechaun.

"Speak up, and tell me where you've hidden the gold!" demanded Ninny Nanny, shaking him till his wee head wobbled.

"The river," squawked the leprechaun. "I put it under the river!"

"Sure, and I'm not believing that. How did you get it under the river? And how am I to get it out?" asked Ninny Nanny.

"I've told you where, but I'll not tell you how," grumbled the leprechaun.

Ninny Nanny got the bucket and started to bail out the river.
She was tossing water onto the riverbank at a furious rate.

"'Tis witless you are, girl," laughed the leprechaun.
"Can't you see all that water sliding back where it came from?"

And he was right, of course, so Ninny Nanny emptied her bucket
into the water barrel till the barrel was full to overflowing—
but the river was as deep as before. And that was that.

"Sure, and 'tis a liar you are, Leprechaun," wailed Ninny Nanny,
"and 'tis throwing you into the river I am!"

"Don't be hasty, girl," begged the leprechaun.
"A liar I'm not, just forgetful at times. I remember clearly now.
I buried my treasure in your very own potato patch."

"I'm not believing you, Leprechaun!
  'Tis another lie you're telling me," said Ninny Nanny.

"Then 'tis foolish you are, girl," said the wee man,
"for leprechauns never lie."

"Aye, I've heard tell—they're bound by fairy law
  to tell the truth," said Gram.

"Agh! I'll believe that when I see it,"
  grumbled Ninny Nanny, as she went to fetch the spade.

Ninny Nanny dug and grubbed about in the potato patch.
Gram smiled to see all the potatoes scattered about.
The leprechaun scowled.

Ninny Nanny dug the potato patch wide and deep,
uprooting all but one of the potato plants.
Sure, and all she had to show for her efforts
was a hole in the garden and a heap of potatoes.
And that was that.

She threw down the spade in disgust.
"I've had enough of digging—
and I've had enough of lying leprechauns!" bawled Ninny Nanny.
"Let him loose, Gram, for we'll be needing that sack for potatoes."

So, Gram untied the sack,
and whist, like a shooting star in the night, the wee man vanished.

Ninny Nanny and Gram supped on good, hot, hearty potato soup
and then fell soundly asleep in their warm, dry hut—

while out in the potato patch
the wee leprechaun was busily digging up the last potato plant.
He carefully lifted out his pot of gold, muttering,
"Aye, leprechauns never lie,"
as he trotted off to find a safer hiding place.

And that was that!

4/98